Maxwell's Rainbow

Acknowledgements

Some of these poems have appeared in *Poetry Ireland Review, The New Writer, Other Poetry, Ambit* and *The North*. 'Maxwell's Rainbow' was a runner up in the 1998 Arvon International Poetry Competition and published in the Arvon Anthology, *The Ring of Words*. 'Terra Firma' and 'Genes' are from *All Things Bright*, a performance piece commissioned in 1999 by Signposts, the Sheffield Writers Development Project. 'The Devil's Arse' was written with support from The Opening Line project. 'Protestations of Innocence' is from *Moonlight and Magnetism*, a performance funded by a Royal Society Millennium Award, 1999. 'Project Phoenix', a collaboration with William Neil, composer, was premièred and broadcast in Chicago 2001 and recorded by Chicago Pro Musica.

Thanks to Dr. Ian Morrison at Jodrell Bank for making time to talk to Diana Syder about SETI, also to Sune Joergensen of the Tvind organisation in Denmark, for introducing her to William Neil.

Previous publications
Hubble, Smith/Doorstop Books
The Blue Bang Theory (with John Sewell, Colin Sutherill and Terry Gifford), Redbeck Press
Catching the Light, Slow Dancer
Folding the Map, Rotherham Arts.

Diana Syder has received a Public Awareness of Science Award from the Institute of Physics for her poetry and is currently a Leverhulme artist in residence at the Department of Electronic and Electrical Engineering, University of Sheffield.

Maxwell's Rainbow

Diana Syder

Smith/Doorstop Books

for Martin

and

Colin, Kev, Terry, John, David, Liz, Ann, and Ian

Published 2002 by
Smith/Doorstop Books
The Poetry Business
The Studio
Byram Arcade
Westgate
Huddersfield HD1 1ND

ISBN 1-902382-38-2

British Library Cataloguing-in-Publication Data. A catalogue
record for this book is available from the British Library.

Typeset at The Poetry Business
Printed by Peepal Tree, Leeds
Cover picture used by kind permission of NASA (McClintock
& M. Garcia)
Author's photo by Stefan Perkins

For representation and distribution, in first instance contact
the publishers: tel 01484 434840, fax 01484 426566, email
edit@poetrybusiness.co.uk

The Poetry Business gratefully acknowledges the help of
Kirklees Metropolitan Council and Yorkshire Arts.

CONTENTS

Newton's Laws

What the greatest scientific mind of all time
didn't know or couldn't work out,
wasn't worth knowing, it was said

but Newton was a virgin when he died
and never discovered the mass of another's body,
its inertia at rest, the way it responds

to external forces, or the force a body
experiences when it interacts with another
body, an inclination, the initial uphill effort

building towards a few slow seconds
of weightlessness, then free fall
and an easy acceleration all the way down.

The Expansion of Gases

I have begun to understand the excitation
of a gas molecule as it rushes to fill a vacuum
because although I'm happy in a small house
open space changes my behaviour entirely.

It happens on a big lawn, wanting to run
wild till I reach a steady state of dancing,
or getting to yoga early and the empty hall
an invitation to spread my arms and fly into it,
at the very least to do my postures wholeheartedly,
without banging into things, like a bird might.

When you say them aloud, there are even
some words that are empty except for tall clouds
boiling overhead, such as *steppe* and *savannah*.
On an open road my pulse accelerates past signs
to The North and any hot moorland day
lark song evaporates me into high-pressure blue.

Come night time, when I close my eyes,
a shred of last night's dream wafts past
and before I fall asleep there's just long enough
to have a picture of myself going for the ultimate

in some far-fetched chemistry where I'm on
my own in deepest space, dancing past the stars
with my arms wide, head back, giving it
everything I've got and laughing out loud.

Flight

Speed. West to East as the crow flies.
In the cockpit, the horizon tilting.
Ease her round, the engine's intonation rises
and the sun comes up easy. Full sunburst.
Level out. On course for the day.

A jet of gas breaks from the sun's corona,
spurts thousands of miles into space.
You can't see it but you know it happens,
like the energy in you that wants to accelerate
in all directions, full throttle, straight, true,
with just for once nothing in the way of it.

Summit

The believer comes to be nearer the sky
and it's no surprise that God's made a mountain
for him to stand on because he's special
to God, he knows it beyond doubt.
The mountain is evidence of greater things,
so he prays, in places like this, for revelation.

The unbeliever can see the quick of everything
from up here and be part of it at will by standing still.
His own atoms are joining in right now
and he's glad he belongs, is small
enough not to matter too much,
because what he sees from here is a miracle.

Natural Philosophy

for Richard Dawkins

Twelve statues gather in a circle
round the Philosopher's Pool
like creatures come to drink.

For two hundred years,
their classical heads
have reflected in the water,
intent, as if they hope to learn
something and the slightest
occurrence might be significant.

What they have discovered is that –
though a water lily opening,
the visit of a bird, a breeze
or rain breaking up the picture,
seem to be allowed –
it's against the laws
of nature for a statue to move
so it's vital that they don't

because one intake of breath
would ruin everything.

Genes

I've only to look at my parents:
my mother's face, I'm told, also arms, breasts.
My father's height, legs and ankles.

And personality's easy according to her
with all the bad traits coming from him.

Health is grim ... glaucoma
and back problems strong
on the long-lived, maternal side
and though my father was healthier
as a going enterprise there's angina
and ulcers on both sides.

I'm me!
I yelled at seventeen, desperate
to claim some independent features.

More so now, as the present
pours faster and faster through me
and what's gone before begins to come true.

I'm a hybrid, fighting all my fates
and piecing together one future.

Terra Firma

Long ago, at the start of all things,
the beasts line up along the shingle
as they come, two by two, out of the ocean.
There's a north wind and it is cold
as far as the eye can see.

Last of all, the blind, hump-backed brute
of evolution heaves himself out, stands
like a lost dog on the strand, howling with hunger,
not understanding what it's all about,
where he's come from or where he's going to.

In the distance, a faint bell summons
the naked world to begin and the footsteps
of all things coming to be firmly set in clay.

And then the dogged creature of evolution,
with no opinions about any of it, staggers
clumsily back into the shallows and slips
below the surface like the sinking sun.

I've walked onto the land forever,
look back at what's out of sight
from the beach, like what's out of reach
in people's eyes, mysteries below the surface,
the bottomless fathoms where the ancestors
had their day and it all continues.

As for the elemental laws that are waiting for me
at the end of the sky, their turn will come.
Meanwhile, this is my Eden. You're in it.

The Cell

Think of a time-lapse city
in less than the space of a pinpoint.
Enter it through an outer wall
that is fluid with the hustle
of import and export.

Watch mitochondria
manufacturing high-energy
phosphate bonds and go right up
to ribosomes knitting amino acids
onto slinky protein strings.

In the nucleus, wander through
the back streets of your chromosomes
and finger their gigabytes of memory,
where whatever information
was written at the start
is what your heart lives with.

Kneel among the molecules
as they crowd round to exchange atoms
and accept with open arms whatever
is given to you about the world
you're growing older with.

Go ever deeper into the city.
All by itself it is a true miracle.

Don't pray to anything less.
Bow your head and study the cell.

Tropic

The sun flogs its vicious weight
across deserts, stony hills,
deep city streets, touches the man
on his slog up the mountain,
strips beaches, rainforest,
snowy plateaux, sears grassland,
meadows, ripens and splits
the full seeded earth
till the earth's back bleeds.

Moisture comes, summoned
from wells and water tables,
deep bore holes, lakes, the skin
peeled from estuaries and oceans,
puddles, ponds, whole rivers gone,
lifted clean off the ground
and my body obliges.

Deep inside the liquids rise,
obey their laws of salt and saliva
with a slippery upper lip, wet eyelids.
Water pools in the basin of my neck
and sweat evaporates from the back
of my knees till I am burned off,
sucked up and out, my skin wide open.
No choice. There will be no trace.
I lie naked on the bed and let it happen.

The overhead sun is a burning tree.
Layer by layer the sun drinks me,
year by year I drink the sun.

Yoga

for Barbara

This is the bird posture
      the cobra
           the cat.

This is the twisted warrior
          the moon
              the heron
            stooping.

Here is a perfectly flat inland lake
      and in the prayer position
           the sea is calling.

Here is the dancer
          undressed.

Or snow at dawn.
      on a single cherry tree.

I want death
      to be this
      cut-loose-and-floating
         feeling,

that speck
         soaring.

Protestations of Innocence

after The Book of the Dead

Here am I. I have come to thee
in the Hall of Righteousness
that I may be released from all my sins.

O Thou who Recycles
> I have not wasted paper or glass since 1990.

O Multiplier of Microbes
> I have not been houseproud.

O Giver of Ecstasies
> I have not taken mood enhancers, unless you count
> caffeine.

O Raveller of DNA
> I have not been unfaithful to any current partner.

O Thou Opener and Shutter of Doors
> I have not wasted opportunities.

O Roller-skating, Hang-gliding One
> I have not been sluggish, except during my period.

O Weigher of Scales
> I have not taken what was not mine, except used
> envelopes.

O Thou of Steady Liver
> I have not taken alcohol, except as is consistent with a
> reduction in the risk of diseases of the heart.

O Pacific One
> I have not killed, except for mosquitoes, fleas,
> grasshoppers and bacteria, also indirectly sheep, cows,
> chickens and fish of culinary varieties.

O Right and Left Handed God
> I have been neither Capitalist nor Communist.

O Thou of the Pure Garden
> I have not used slug pellets.

O Nester of Jackdaws
> I have not cowled my chimney pots.

O Speaker of Curses
    I have not been bad tempered, except just before my
    period.
O Wearer of Masks
    I have not concealed my true face, unless I judged it
    to be in everyone's best interest.
O Universal One
    I have not been perfect but tried my best.

I honour you. Be kind to my spirit.
Let the Boatman guide me through the firmament
of Yesterday, Today and Tomorrow,
to rest forever in your emptiness.

Wet Withers

  stone circle, Derbyshire

We all agreed to come, separately, this winter.
One of you could have just stepped out of sight
as I breasted the shoulder of the hill,

your trails could be not yet made or wet and long cold.
I don't know but make a point of saying hello
to your ghosts, one at a time, standing here.

Also to the ghost of Bronze Age man with his head cold,
shivering and fevered but coming anyway
because it was expected, because he'd said he would.

I sneeze, it's bitter, the moor's sopping wet
and because it was an effort to get here
I want it to be worth the trip – Ringinglow,

Stanage, Bleaklow and the whole of the Dark Peak
laid out with midsummer sunrise sighted over Higgar Tor
and midwinter moonrise from a pillar on Burbage Moor –

but the wind chill inside's blowing me hot and cold.
I can't think of anything but getting back
to a good fire, whisky, warm dry feet. I sneeze again.

No matter how many people have made their way
to this point and looked out or waited, for all the world
whenever I stand here I am First. And Last.

Succession on East Moor

As far back as I can remember, the grassland
either side of the Roman Road was blonde waters
bending to the wind on a choppy day.

It could have been anywhere for all I knew then,
an open ocean or a plateau running along the top
of the world, the possibilities open and endless.

When the shrubs came it was just as I imagined
the Australian bush, uprooted and replanted here
with wallabies, parrots, the occasional gum tree.

Then as shrubs became saplings, the road was a track
across an African savannah in which acacia trees
would not have been out of place, nor a band of ostrich.

Now hazel and rowan have grown up tall
and what's been established is largely how it will be
from now on, anything new will have to compete

for what light and space is left and the view
can never again be so clear to the horizon.
Outliving a landscape makes me older than the hills.

Maxwell's Rainbow

*the electromagnetic spectrum, from short to long
wavelength: gamma rays, x-rays, ultraviolet, visible light,
infrared and radio.*

Gamma rays

No substance.
Just a sly
downpour
from the sky

an uncommon
vibration
you can't see,
quicksilver
as the gap

between what's said
and what's meant
but then it's gone
and you can't ever
put your finger on it.

Such gauzy
stuff can't break
our bones but it does
make changes
in DNA:

the story
of the first ever
corkscrew willow
found growing
outside Hiroshima;

the odds for
and against misshapes
or being the wrong
side of statistics;

the nature of sickness,
how it starts years
before you know.

X-rays

That film of a right hand
playing the piano,
its macabre grace
revealed to the naked eye
as blackened bones
and a wedding ring

as though it had passed
through fire and all
that's left are the bare
bones and the foggy
outline of arpeggios
articulating themselves.

Ultraviolet

At the end of winter my blue-eyed,
fair-skinned friend is down in the dumps.
Sad. He can't explain why, he just is,
huddles close as he can to his lightbox,

watching the skyline glow through all
the luminous spaces of the copper beech
and waiting for the days to lengthen.

By midsummer he's sunbathing
and looking out through sunspecs.
Too much exposure irritates
his northern skin, spills straight
to the basal layers of his animal fears
till his hairs rise up on end, but taking
the glasses off doesn't restore anything
because, for a minute, the garden
is much brighter than it should be.

Visible light

Last night a friend died and something came undone,
like a hole softly opening in the ozone layer
or the vague unease of an unglazed window.

And so today the world is less safe than it was yesterday,
more sad and mysterious, but even while I'm wondering
if I live my own life well enough, the moon comes full,

daffodils stand unearthly in it and when a moth dives into
my headlamps on the way home, it is a short-lived fleck
of light, whose sudden life is a basic property of night.

Infrared

Mid-morning and my cat's outside on his back in the sun,
limbs splayed out and letting go, eyes shut and I swear it
smiling, on the first, malnourished day of spring.

The earth's warming up like a stone, the expansion
of elements happening smoothly as if the entire planet
were taking up more room and its core smells different,
the skin of the earth giving way, unfastening and letting
things through as though an underworld were swelling
up through this one, the unseen bald white tips
of it crashing through into ours and growing green.

And we love it, lay ourselves flat on the grass
and soak up the sun, having the best of both worlds
and leaving heat maps on the ground after dark
on those rare summer days and nights that are close
as we get to any real evidence for a warm-blooded heart.

Radio

Long ripples coming in, enough time between each crest to
turn over, fall asleep and sink down past ... 2 a.m. ... 3
a.m. ... .4 ... plenty of time to dream an ocean with wide
winged birds slanting and sliding beneath undulating skies
and coils of seaweed lowering and lifting in a half hearted
tide ... time to listen for the belly flop of water slapping at
fat stones or watch the way the water sparkles, slowly, how
the mist comes, everyone dreaming or dreamed of through a
drift of fog across unknown waters ... everything muffled,
nothing clear, yet hearing from a long way off the limbic
pulse of the self's long loop around the world, every single
morning, something in you making the choice between
coming back or staying always on the other side.

The Second Coming

Jesus is trying to give up God
but it's not something he can wear
special colours or disappear
at certain times of the day for.
There's no set text, no prayers to make
or song, nothing to eat or not eat.

There ought to be, it's a serious business
also, cosmology's moved on
and he wants up to date stories
to tell the children, which,
if he had his say, is what the clergy
would be doing on Sundays –

finding ways to celebrate space-time
and show their love for the laws of gravity,
the unbearable constants, also putting spirit
into a Theory of Mind, fleshing it out
and finding a sacred ecology of the heart
that understands grace in the light of DNA.

He'd do it himself, but though his parents
are long dead, he still hears their voices
in his head and just can't take that final step.

His heart of hearts doesn't tell him what to do.
He waits for a clue, a bolt from the blue
but still nothing happens, not a whisper,
not the tiniest flicker of a glimmer of a hint.

So he's got to work it out for himself
this time, like the rest of us have to.

Town of Bethlehem

Once it was a solo to be sung
by me from the back of the school hall,
wanting to give, to be utterly received
and the words were a shoal
of wonderful glassy fish,
crowding and uncrowding.

Now when I sing
I'm an unruly choir whose members
argue endlessly among themselves.

One of them is a bright-eyed bird
still flying straight
from the mouth of the open song.

Another stands back, unsure,
assumes what's going on is harmless
so joins in, but really yearns for new songs,
ones to put a whole heart into.

There's also the troublemaker
who stomps round the outskirts,
muttering about how the whole thing's a con

but the one with all the high notes
is hardest to deal with, backs off
at the crucial moment as though
these words were tricky nets to foul up in.
She tightens the ocean's throat
until the wonderful glittering fish

are turned into everyday dead fish
with stupid eyes and part of the ocean
suddenly smells sour. Once that's happened
there's nothing left to be sung for.

This one can silence the whole choir,
who stand around, opening and closing
and opening their foolish mouths.

In a Tea Cup

If this were a cup in which all life
thundered and oceans rose and fell,
where continents crowded against
and crushed one another and giant trees
rose from unlikely seeds and swayed
and tossed and later fell to rot and dust,
where lightning forked and fungi
wove their quiet quilts below the grass
in a world blown this way and that,
then this would be my cup of tea.

It's also the answer to everything,
everyday, that can't be beaten or borne.
Putting the kettle on becomes a simple baptism
to warm your fingers against and wash away
the sins of the day, so as you blow gently
across the seas of your own life
to calm it or cool it, you don't know
where you'd be without it.

That's better you say as the trees
grow still and the seas hushed,
because when all's said and done,
tomorrow is a new one and still ahead
are many things to be loved.

The History Game

I'd have been a tea planter's daughter,
taken port out to life on a verandah
in cotton, canvas and silk.

There'd have been a handsome father
to play chess in the evening and chat with
above the trumpeting of elephants,
the clatter of macaques on the roof.
Later, woodsmoke and music,
servant's faces, the sibilance of strangers.

I'd have done my best with the insects,
no doubt adjusted to the water eventually
and in frocks and jodhpurs dealt gracefully
with dowagers who called round to tea.

I'd have respected the wisdom of the east,
learned names, customs, greetings
and been kind to the servants
who I taught to read and write
without ever mentioning the King
or English history, even when I was homesick,
because I'd have utterly disapproved of Empire.

I wouldn't have succumbed to fever or the heat
but kept through it all, an English Rose
complexion and been extraordinarily pretty.

That's how it would have been.

Time of the Month

My breasts are melons. I've cut my finger,
burnt tonight's tea and can't string
two thoughts together coherently,
but when a brass band does something patriotic
in a documentary, I crumple in genuine sobs.

Stomach ache, back ache, headache are all one.
Martin tells me, trying to be helpful,
that I've spent six years menstruating, did I realise?
And do I want honey or marmalade on the toast,
which is too difficult. I don't know.
Yesterday I ate a packet of Hob Nobs in one go.

I've tried thinking of goddesses,
moon juice, descending deep
into my Anima and making the most of flux.
I've done mind over matter and Evening Primrose,
none of which beats a hot water bottle,
a pack of Nurofen and a good book.

So count me out of parascending,
partying till dawn, forget the mountain biking,
the gym, the valiant smile, just leave me
to my tantrum, to sulk and cry a lot.

One day I'll get a shed for the bottom
of the garden, retire to it, unclean,
for a week of talking to no one,
with meals brought down on a tray
so I can stare all day at the ceiling
and do bugger all in my menstrual hut.

The Cat and Penny Whistle

It never fails to set her
twining at my ankles
and purring in fifth gear,
then lightly up on the table,
nuzzling her solid little head
against my hands
and on hind legs soft-patting
my mouth, cheek, chin.

This bad tempered creature
turns all kitten drooly
and follows me eagerly
as if I might lead her
to some mouse-ridden place
where woolly jumpers are left
out by radiators all day long.

Oh, the places we might go
if I were not so stubbornly human,
if I were a door she could push against
to open and music were a way
of asking for something,
a way of breaking through.

The Bird Garden

It was just stories twining themselves together,
how, at the heart of our village, was a hidden garden.

First, birds, that their calling kept the neighbours awake
twenty or thirty years ago.
Then exotics, a toucan 'the sorry, lost thing' and parrots.

Later, a monkey and people coming from all over
to see a botanical garden that's nowadays a jungle.

Finally, sitting out one summer Sunday afternoon
drinking wine and then more wine, being asked again,
had I seen it, the magic garden because I ought to,
that the old gate round the corner is the best way in.

                    *

Kew: The Evolution House,
a mock-up of The Garden as it was
in Pre-Cambrian times; fibreglass rock,
otherwise nothing much happening.
One step and the Cambrian era
has steam puffing from vents
and somehow they've done a deep-down
red glow, a lava flow and anaerobic
goings-on in a puddle of mud.

Further along the algae begin.
Around a Silurian pool *the ancestors
of all our plants appear* – they talk
like that, as if it were an explanation.

The liverworts, horsetails and giant ferns
take us on through to the Carboniferous
where a dragonfly big as a chicken clings

to a trunk decaying in a stagnant pond.
The coal measures are laid down.

Halfway now and while we're stroking
the bark of cycads there are scrapes
and screams of aerial things
and on the floor a trail of three-toed prints
is obviously leading somewhere ...

*

Does it have to be grass?
Does there need to be anything natural
at all or is it what the earth gives, just that,
so you could have a garden of metal, plastic
and glass or would this be something different,
change versus staying the same or changing
slowly and a degradation at that?

France. Relief parties in the 1st World War
going out and finding the grass bleached white.
Or men marooned on the hill who watched it
come rolling in below them, what could have been
so much mist on an ordinary morning
lining the valley but this was so much
heavier than air, hideous and rising.

What men do to grass and to each other ...
I think of survivors holding that and living with it
ever after, that now we all have to.

*

I've never come across anywhere like my garden
for sudden calm, the way it hangs so pointedly still.
Even the cat will pause mid-stride then carry on
as if the flow of time were stopping
and starting itself or nothing really *had* happened

and because this time of year is so beautiful,
there *is* a God if I'm not careful, if I forget
to remind myself that we're bound to take
pleasure in what we've evolved with,
to treasure what we know, also what we make.

We make our sorrows. I know that,
but this time of year what I can't get away from
is that *it is* 'beautiful' – high summer piled
upon high summer so each year the word grows
past itself and the world surpasses its own meaning.

And every year I say *I have never appreciated*
until now, the way light coming through poppies
lasers straight to the heart and colours everything.
It also happens with green and blue.

Light is a dangerous thing for a non-believer.

                    *

Through fusty darkness and the innards of shrubs
into broad daylight and open-ended lawns.

This is from childhood – not our grass, we didn't have any,
somewhere else, any green I could get hold of –
either way, what hits me is the same imperative to dance,

arms wide out and up with no fear of breaking
or banging into things, dry grass stippling the soles
of my feet and only the occasional stone to be wary of.

For hours and hours of it, unstoppable,
the music streaming in my head.
I was well aware of the curves and shapes
I made against my mind's eye but beyond that,
more, arms and legs repeating themselves,

willing my heart to burst and for everyone else to go
home and let me dance by myself in a big garden.

*

I've been to the gate,
sun and shade tangled together
across a single path leading in.

I swear there was the call
of what could have been a toucan, possibly,
the rattle of tree tops as it flew somewhere
and then another cry and one more,
clean at the edges as though emerging
from a great space or a great silence.

*

GUIDE TO THE BIRD GARDEN

Do not put your fingers through the mesh.

Note the beautiful flight
of the Red-crested Touraco
and the call of the Go-away bird.
The Toucans are fed on
artificial nectar and live fruit flies.
Flamingos are happy in snow.
Humming birds are aggressive.

Please close all gates.

*

It happens like this: dark even on a sunny day,
grasses and nettles are chin-high, goosegrass is treacherous.
Saplings sprout beneath my feet and fast as I tread them down
they spring again making each step claim and trespass.

Bulrushes spike the margins of a lake long gone
and the air's close with elder about to flower.
Overhead the canopies rattle and shush with each liftoff
and landing but a sense of birds escapes me.

The back of the Jubilee Chapel is without light or grace
and a chicken wire fence high as a tennis court is crammed
with trees I can't see the wood for.   I'm up to my neck
in what's tangled and prolific and can't follow

the twists of a single stem, a simple line of thought.
There's no place that dark cannot make fearful and I could never
spend the night here, so it's a relief to find the gate and see
where I'm walking in the common-sense light-of-day street.

What did I expect? Some paradise place, some fabulous fruit?
Perhaps a clearing, in which a gorgeous idea would stand
revealed, one that would shed light on everything around it,
or a time or a place where I could have completely opened.

Oh, something does happen in there, but not something
to be come across like a common-or-garden flower, more
to do with how greenery affirms itself, what is revealed
or hidden from one year's end to the next, or takes place

when no one's watching. In the same way, what there is
of solace, pools in my own heart and evolves there,
so it's essential to tread quietly because the nearer
I get to this, the more I might let the green that is in me

grow wherever it wants, the more I might understand
the unforgiving heart of the garden in which I live
and the endless fierce imperative of all the paradise gardens
becoming themselves and flowering for no reason.

The Earth Factory

Blue Circle Cement Works, Hope Valley, Derbyshire

The factory builds itself before your eyes
as though some Futurist dreamed
of simple cylinders and monumental blocks.

Conveyor belts traffic overhead,
there's the crunch of chippings underfoot
and everything's grey with cement dust.
Steam pours from silos, tanks and vents.
Spare parts are strewn around like giant meccano
or the bits of a clock; a gear, a spring,
an escapement, rods as thick as an oak tree.
You can see how it all fastened together,
the nuts and bolts of time and motion.

A twig pokes at you
as if there's something you ought to remember.
Celandines among the birches are a hint,
the beginnings of an idea or something alien
and ivy points the way to the great quarries,
a thousand feet of limestone laid wide open,
whole epochs of geological time blasted
into boulders and carted away.

A JCB grinds its gears out of sight,
dumps a load of thunder that breaks
into smaller and smaller pieces
till a final pebble rocks to a stop.
The magic of gravity! One chunk falling
on another, a whole life mounting up
one stone at a time but barely chance
to focus on it before it's come to a standstill.

The place is deserted, plenty
going on but no-one doing it.
A workforce of six hundred men
and you never get to see them,
as though some narcotic spell keeps
everything in a stupor of morphia,
lithium and the heavy metals of sleep.

You assume a control room,
a clean area where artificial light
pools on a polished floor and ranks
of buttons keep it all going
with occasional adjustments
to the balance and counterbalance.

It's the sort of elemental set
that good and bad would get
to fight it out in, action and reaction
in an old film or a simple system.

Overhead, the chimney's a white
colossus against the blue sky.
Someone in the village said,
when he was coming in to land,
the smoke was what he looked for first
and when he saw that, he was home.

On a calm day it's a prayer
heading straight up through the stratosphere
and out, more or less on a direct line
to heaven, that much of it and so shining
white on a sunny day you'd swear
it was pure enough to get there.

On the ground 50,000 volts keep the dust
emissions down, earth into the valley.
Two rotary kilns are 70 metres long,
wide as a house tumbling round at 1.7 revs
a minute, 24 hours a day.
                Or is it …
the movement of the earth you can hear,
the great axles fixed and the hills rotating?
Also the sky.

A thrush sings its heart out.
A clear thought drops into place:
this is the engine that cranks the earth
through space, steers it past night and day,
also gears the orbits, the almighty spirals
and powers up the stars.

Which means seasons of villages and cities
are decided here, from here the equinoxes
are fixed, the millennia carried out,
even the very nature of immense darkness
is anchored to this valley, where the axle turns.

Now the earth is swung towards the sun.
Underground, rabbits feel the pulse
and quiver softly, crouch close as they can
to the workings of the exquisite heart.

        *

By night, brilliant sodium light.
Steam transmuted to gold dust.
Everything lit up as if the Starship Enterprise
were docked here. Shield your eyes
and if you feel compelled to speak at all,
use a hushed voice, like in a cave, or cathedral.

A freight train rattles through the wood.
Badgers forage by the track
and up on the hill, lambs shimmer
with a phosphorescent sheep dip
that scares off foxes.

And now the moon's up
you can't drag your eyes away.
What's fluid in you, leans.
The water table lifts beneath your feet
and rock waves of anticline and syncline
strain in different directions along
the crazy highroads of strata and seam.

In this weird light, the cavernous door
of the new coal store has the pull
of a local black hole, which for all you know,
could lead straight down to the deepest pit of all.
Getting too close means never to escape
or perhaps mistaking a far off truck's
reversing bleat for the falling note
of someone whose courage failed
when their time came and didn't want to go.

Your own last whimper will fade
to the final sound of all the languages ever.
Noises issuing from the mouths of water and rock
and even the stopped mouths of the dead
and the extinct will catch up with you.

You too will join the swollen statements
of underground streams pouring
into the ocean, the teeming ocean
that whispers itself into the troubled dreams
of the living, who may or may not hear,

who are busy weeping their own tears
into a sea where it all still matters
and into which, from time to time,
the bell drops its reminders.

Further down still and nothing to do with men,
molten iron pitches, tumbles and churns
in the furnace that rolls the planet round.

Now you've been here, go home.
Leave by the back way, find your way back
to a world where time's a thing to run out of

and take a stone from the track to remind you
of rocks, boulders, gravel, dust – the necessary
business of grinding into manageable pieces
what seems boundless, cause and effect, effort
and the resounding avalanche of our industry.

The Devil's Arse

Peak Cavern, Castleton

Jackdaw

His voice is a hammer on the cliff,
sore on the throat, scrapes down
to the bone, a sudden storm in which
everything rattles and drops sharp as stone.

His flight is vertigo, an abyss
into which the hill folds and night falls.
He has battled for the branch
he now rides like a captain,
feels for the air with his wingtips,
prises apart its splits and faults
till he slips between and once more
slides over deep green oceans
of chestnut and sycamore.

His heart is a sooty flame
that nothing has opened.
His will pours wave after wave
against the raw cliff face.
Swooping close and low he enters
the old earth, origins, slow water.

Farther in than words, thoughts,
he is a thousand hooded birds
whose hard-edged sound
unsettles the stony silences.

Titan

This year a new void was discovered
far beyond where the tourists go.

First it was the biggest
in Derbyshire, then taller
than Gaping Gill, now you can fit
Hope Valley Cement Works chimney
in there with room to spare.

Titan, they've named it,
the Elder gods still teasing us underground –
shot from the bottom and looking up,
a torchlit caver dangles in mid-air
on the end of his piece of string.

Moss, floodlit

See-through stems are swimming in light
and delicate velvet heads sweep bright green perfectly
to the light's edge and no further, grabbing
any chance to grow where it can, while it can.

Two million tons of rock overhead
yet a footstep would flatten it.

Earth to Earth

He's still there,
threaded along a crack
somewhere inside this hill,
the stuck man, his strung bones

slumped in the depths of my imagination
and thin enough to crawl out
easily now, if he'd a mind to.

Beyond the Great Cave

As far as we can go, the flush of water
far below and because, to the Celts,

the air at water sources was numinous,
the division between worlds at its thinnest,

when I screw up my eyes I can picture
the underworld all our tunnels lead to:

a cliff of black limestone is polished smooth
of crag, pinnacle, foothold, crack. Immaculate.

I'm small before it, trying to hold steady
the fixed gaze of the face of darkness,

hoping for a split second shiver of meaning,
some flutter of understanding to balance

at the back of my mind or on the tip
of my tongue but there's no such thing,

no way back and nothing left to hang on to.
Knowing I once overflowed with desires

and warm desolations makes no difference,
even the beautiful boat of the poet

surely cannot stay watertight forever.
The ego swings wide open and its last chasm

is empty as moonlight. So the last word
is spoken, the final guttering flame surrendered.

Even the heart is jettisoned
because beyond this there is nothing to carry,

no home anywhere and no more ever to be learned.
Dark is the true stuff of the universe,

what I must welcome one day, if only
I knew where to begin, so I reach out

to the part of me that will one day
wait alone at the rock face and wish her

this separate dark-winged thought:
that I was always her own best company,

of all of them I was the one who loved her
lifelong and only. I wish for this to settle

on her gently, as some small steadiness
while the grip of the universe

shakes loose from her shoulders
and all creation shudders to a close.

Peake Hole

How could such a dank place ever feel like home?
I ask Stan Cox, caver, because people did live here,
the cave roof's streaked with the soot of their need
to be warm and eat. He says of course,
there's nowhere more welcoming or safer,
that the cavers call it Great Mother Peak and his voice
widens out as he says again *Great Mother Peak*.
I glance at what we've come out of – centuries
of backache, darkness and cold a mile deep.

                    *

My place is easy to love. It is beautiful.
Hills purple to the west every sunset,
sedges flicked in light, sun draped
from the clouds onto pastureland and moors
where I can bask in the pleasure
of finding out what I am and living with it,
love pooling in each footprint
as I make my way home –

how you might talk about art:
Stefan, 16, who's just discovered
it's a real place, somewhere to live in,
talks about a refuge, friend,
and you can tell from that it's no phase
he's going through but somewhere
he'll be trying to get further into all his life.

                    *

For how many tens of thousands of years
have our swifts' fledglings each June
read *here* for north and gone no further?
A thread of imperative with no pictures or words to it,
iron clunking shut onto its magnet,

the small thump of capture and so they are home,
a thin layer of plaster between our limp bodies
and their stuttering baby tongues,
the rustling in the bedroom wall at night
when one and then all of them turn over.

I don't understand this cavernous love.
Somewhere in my heart's chambers
the grass has grown itself greener here,
the houses safer, the bedrock steadier.
And so I am docked, settled with the door shut,
fire lit, kettle on and the immense effort over.

*

Far far ahead, we will stand in our new gardens,
float our hearts on fine tunings into the night sky
and still show our children, who will feel,
without being told, that it is out there,
deathly cold now but so programmed into us
that wherever we go, however far from human we become,
we will carry within us the glowstone that is love
for the ghost of the Earth that was home.

Making Rope

Just inside the cave, a few stubs of houses,
a dingy pub, ropemakers' poles
receding into the darkness
where grey faces watched the rain
and coughed little roses of phlegm
into the smoke as they wound and flexed,
men, women and children taking the strain,
forcing a twist into hundreds of fathoms
of rigging for ships that would break the Armada.

Rope enough to anchor
a landlubber with sore hands
to his rough bed under the thatch.

To me, his seems a miserable life,
half home, half abyss, but he must have made
some sort of peace with darkness,
found underfoot the rockhard bed
of what is heartfelt and slept well in it.

Or maybe his dream
was having a well lit place to migrate to,
every evening dropping the coils
of the day and walking straight
at the gape of the cave mouth.

His life, however grim,
whatever he made of it, is already laid.
I must leave him to what he had,
find the best way to unbind
my own human cry
and set it freely into the wild.

Pilgrim

We are going in the same direction
at roughly the same speed as strangers,
a river with our own confluences,
we nod, we smile, we carry on.

Up the narrow path we come
our dark waters streaming from the hills

and villages, bringing lanterns.
We are small flames carried downstream.

The time of year doesn't matter,
this is just the time that has been agreed.
It doesn't matter what we sing,
because no words say what we are
singing about, these are just words
that have been agreed upon.

The tune is not important
as long as it is old enough
to be in our bones.

So I am singing with 3,000 people
and a brass band underground.
Let the earth make of this what it will.

Shocks and aftershocks,
our song a fist against
unaccountable tons of rock,
higher and harder

O come all ye faithful
till the roof is a lake,
a mirror, a night sky riding
on a sound deep and strong
enough to open limestone

and the great door of myself.

Now we are singing.

The Edges

Curbar Gap, Sunset

The electricity of height.
Revealed, the far hills' density,
the field-strength of greens,
heather on full pulse, the smoking wire
of a lapwing's cry across frayed grasses
with every blade a thorn of light.

When I move, the earth's magnetic field
affects my own, generates a cunning
voltage that connects me to this place
with little shocks of tenderness,
all the domains of my heart satisfied.

Steep sky greys are dark as a bird's wing.
Flames in the clouds are a charge on the hill.
Power surges through the tree
and gritstone glints, each grain coming
into its own as the wall conducts
the current west to Shining Tor, Shutlingslowe,
Chrome Hill and on around the world.

At the end of wall, cliff, hill, a silence
into which gorse blasts its panoramic fanfare
and a blackbird spills its last *gloria* of the day.

Snow, Eyam Edge

Clouds pour out of heaven
onto Longstone Edge,
hilltop and heavy air rolled into one.
A blast of white and the ground

has dropped away to all
these blank, astounding distances.

To the south, the world ends
in a doom of smoke and snow
pillowing behind Chesterfield.

Northward, the lemon silver light
is a great lake lapping the rim of the parted clouds,
a sky giftwrapped and opened up
into something unfrozen, beyond,
to be walked into or turned
towards with a vaulting heart.

It doesn't come plainer
than this epic of dark and light.
Up here, nothing hides or is hidden,
my span is endless,
the balance right,

as the eye of the universe
turns tender for a moment
above the creaking cradle of earth.

Trying on Wings, Stanedge

Numbness first, then tingling,
strange nerves playing up
just under the skin, irritable,
full of prickle, then pain
jabbing straight through
my shoulder blades to just below
my breast bone. Budding.

My neck tenses to take the strain.
My toes are ready, eyes shut,
arms high-pitched
and feeling for the wind.

I never get further than this.

White Edge

I can see why the ancestors thought
there had to be somewhere else
and where the pearly gates came from –
their golden edge is the frosted lemon lip
of the parting clouds and seen through that gap
the silvery sky is a gift or an invitation.

Even now, angels might lean any moment
through the shining hole, reach low enough
to clasp my wrist and pull me through,
noble faces smiling, breath steaming,
cheeks flushed with the exertion of stooping
into our weighty world. 'Here' one might say,
'A shortcut, let me help.' as he sets
a golden ladder to my feet and I step forward
ready to scorch my hands on its purity.

For a moment I wish it was like that,
a place that might be searched for
and travelled into, a precious valley
where a great creature burns like the sun.

Then I take a deep breath and choose
the real world, its dark clouds, bitter winds
and perfect, earthbound sky.

Froggatt Edge

A hard climb through to the end of winter.
An iridescent beetle pivots up and down
the cliffs of someone's footprint in the mud.
Ferns white-knuckle through last year's leaf.
Hawthorns snake from the ground
and a clump of snowdrops is caught
out in the open by a patch of sun.

Something startles in the underbrush.
Stock still, I search the shadows, check
over my shoulder but the time-lapse ivy
has crept in behind and smothered
all the footsteps I ever made climbing up this hill.

Sweating now and breathing hard on leaf gas.
A thrush strings rococo scales among the trees.
A hill-sheep stands its ground. My breath
is the full drag of sap lifted root lip to leaf tip.

A last tree sighs out and I surface
onto the moor, unfold and evert myself,
hands first, longer limbs unrolled,
the deepest organs carefully unpacked
and the whole moist factory
of myself laid open to the sky.

The wind rips away all the old skins
of the morning and I am one more
living creature basking on a ledge.

Burbage Rocks, Ringinglow

moon

Its slow traverse
of the cliff face
has entered the rock
as a slight unsettling
of electrons
to the right or left,
a rhythm of quartz.

The moon as a dull lamp
in deep stone
tugging at the dead weight
of bedrock

or a pulse
through water-filled seams
with molecules dragged
one way and then the other
by a harsh moon sea
casting its shadows

or an afternoon moon
chased silver blue against
the chalky flats of the sky.

The moon prints itself.
The moon prints itself

is how moon is remembered.

rain

Rock shines.
Water as a way to listen.
Echo spatters on echo
and slams in clouds
down the valley.

The driven rain dissolves
elephantine greys,
waterlogged clays,
an entire serene
and plodding chemistry
of endurances
in which crystals
are translated
into sinuous currents.

Deltas of water
flood and drain.

Run off and spate,
how rain is remembered.

wind

Clamour and fracture,
a major to minor shift
in the shriek of gullies
and cloughs, barbed wire
and broken fences.

With the storm at full height,
all the muscles
of the valley grab at it,
slab upon slab
of noise tumbles down
from the turbulence
of open country

then dropping
out of the wind,
the cliff's sudden silences.

Rib bones rock on the turf,
a section of spine strung
between reed clump and heather.
Scraps of fleece and sheep shit
catch in the cracks
where grit scours nooks
and crannies deeper.

By the grind of sediment
is wind remembered.

cliff

I am outcrop, edge, crack,
ledge, overhang, gully,
sheer face, slab and cleft.
I am rubble and scree,
wet grit, gravels
and coarse blown sand.
This occupies me.

The filmy universe flies past
or undone by the evening sun
I melt in the distance.

Moon is a ghost,
midnight a blue chill
scratched onto silicates.
Morning is a sheer drop.

The massive epochs
are gathered behind.

I lean into the day.

Project Phoenix

> *This 5 year project has checked 1,000 stars in our galaxy for evidence of intelligent life.*

Listen to a thousand stars,
like washing for gems with greedy fingers
on the fringes of a brilliant ocean no-one knows
the true depths or other side of.

Scan a speckled TV screen
for the frequency of the hydrogen atom,
like closing your eyes and listening
to heavy snow spinning from a wintry sky.

                    *

Alone or not?
Either beggar belief when even
a lifeless universe would be amazing
so try it all ways:

what if complexity and mind
are predestined as a peculiar constant
of space-time, with the universe
a teeming carnival of civilisations
all eager to hear from us, or more likely
that we might hear from, an impact
that would ring the planet like a bell.

Even today on the moor,
alien histories might smash through
my skin, shake the heather and saturate
the peat while I feel a torrent of nothing.

We can already say we're the only humans;
with no DNA in common
nothing out there is ever likely to enjoy
the colour of my eyes, skin, the shapes
of my appendages, nor I its,
hard enough most of the time
to feel at one with myself
let alone the rest of creation –
I am so far from understanding
even the world of my best friend –
sometimes the heart's galactic separations.

How did our slippery cells ever come
to be born among balls of gas colliding?
The hell fire furnace turned up full
with time and heat stretched out in all directions,
a rush of horizons becoming the centre
of our galaxy and the insane pull of gravity
pounding outward from a singularity.
                              Dot.
            Or the first microbe
spinning its endless proteins
into megatons of interplanetary plankton.
Life at its simplest hanging motionless
in the quirky fathoms of space
with superbugs buried deep
in the rocks of ice-locked moons.

If complexity *is* rare,
the result of fluctuations
in the fundamentals from one part
to another, then we're an anomaly
in the giddy ways of space-time
and the worth of every creature
rockets sky high; my cat

is doubly precious, a termite gains
irreducible worth and the man
on the bus is a crucial geometry
to be added to the sum of the universe.

Far-fetched, but some days
I look back through the narrow gates
of chance and glimpse the real odds against us –
a long trail of burning bridges,
their fires dimming to the distance
and the earliest years already cold

and then it seems all but certain
that when the heather quivers,
it's no more than the wind
bending the pale moor grass,
bending the tiny hairs in my cochlear,
that beyond the outermost orbits
of the heart, all its moments of death,
moments of tenderness
                              there is no-one.

    Raw silence.

    The universe collapses
    to a factor of one.

    I fall forever.

    The sun thunders on.

Or am I flying?
My present tense is omnipotent,
sinks to my shoulders like a coat
embroidered with the powers of carbon,

the glories of the great interstellar gas pillars,
their hydrogen and helium nuclei
all shot through with photons
and the astrochemistry of dust

but also edged with origins
and what the ancestors endured
to put me here. Each desperate day
of theirs makes an epic freight,
my knees buckle under the tonnage
of being so unique and I wonder
what on earth's in store if nothing else,
anywhere, has done it before?

                    *

Too late. Science trumpets its ideas.
They wheel like hawks over our heads
and each year fly higher, straight
at the stark white fires of all possible stars.
A single feather falls from each.
                                    Fire and ice.

Again and again the incandescence,
as more and more of it falls into place.
And sometimes I stagger back
as though it were dangerous to watch
or stand open-mouthed, stupid,
as if the whole thing were dreamed
inside a cave long ago.

But surely, any creature that is born
from the ash of suns, builds a telescope,
predicts a lunar eclipse and waits up for it,
is excited, elated, consumed with longing
at the sight and homesick –

surely such a creature is well-equipped
to cope with a fallout of wonders.

                *

Night comes
and with it a fine-tuned sense
of apple trees being nocturnal.

Alone or not?

I argue the toss on our flat roof.
An owl sings across deep fields
wanting more of itself.

Across chaos and endless zeros
the universe attached itself to me
nine months before my birth.
Now I cling on tight, trembling often
yet swollen hopelessly with love
for every last particle and wave.

        There is nothing I know
        only the expanse,
        nothing I want more
        than the expanse to enter.

The sky cracks,
the moment torn apart
as a garden speeds past
the present and all roads
to the future are closed.

It is the world I live in that owns me,
in which I bear witness like a drunk,
all sorrow, all joy.

I am a source deep in space.

The apple trees fail to get the point
but the rapturous faces of lilies
crowding in the moonlight
insist that now we're here,
what's been started must be fulfilled.

From way beyond the almost perfect vacuums
a universe looks me straight in the eye

       silence   within silence.

The Lovell Telescope, Jodrell Bank

for Staff Withington and Ian Morrison

*Arecibo is the 56 million channel receiver in Puerto Rico
involved in SETI (the Search for Extra Terrestrial
Intelligence). That part of the spectrum between 18-
21cm is where we are most likely to find signals and
known as the Waterhole Band.*

Friesians graze the field, heraldic.
A beetle makes slow progress
across the slippery dish of the cosmos
while crows plot a straight line home
to roost in Pennine space-time.

I'd forgotten how potent it was, close to,
filling the sky with grids and rails,
the white bowl remote and brimming with birdsong.

My brother remembers the wildlife.
He did his PhD here, says what's always
stayed with him from that time
is an abiding sense of how astronomy
gets done in the earth's serene places.

*

What it must be like on a listening night:
the call from Arecibo comes through
about midnight, asking to take over,
then something fibre-optic happens
in a box of tricks on a window sill
and the great dish swings to the south west.

Digital receivers listen hour after hour
in senses we don't possess
for the all-important line emission of hydrogen,
till the once-a-week false alarm tips the system
into second-stage observations and sets the heart
of the man, who tomorrow will fall asleep
in the library, beating a little faster.

In an argument with silence
the cows don't matter.
Nor does the grass.

       *

Caroline, who's just lost her mother
so connections are important,
knows the farmer who sold the land
to the telescope in the first place,
says he's selling the herd in a couple of weeks
and can't think of anything else
but doesn't want visitors
because after three generations
he's too upset to talk about it.

What she liked best, more than the Planetarium,
was going back to the cafeteria, just sitting
for ages beneath the dish with a cup of tea
and looking up, was surprised,
without a physics-bone in her body,
to find it all so moving.

       *

The telescope parked to the zenith
for safety beneath storm clouds.

The sky cracks its bones
and rain erupts
random patterns against us.

*

If I were a potter I'd make bowls, only.
Hundreds and hundreds to be left out in the rain
because for the purest experience of giving or receiving,
what changes hands must have little value,
say sand in a desert, water on an island.

So there we are with our vessels
and faces of longing as the surface swings open.
Stars sway beneath us, mirror into mirror.

Caroline would like to see her mother's face.
I would hope to glimpse something farther off,
whatever comes to be possible, the last drops
of mystery opened out and everything radiant.

Am I empty or full?
Caroline, is she full?
And the farmer, what has the sky given him?
                              Rain, certainly
and the multiple stomachs of cows
in whose tender, weighted udders
have swung Milky Way drifts
of fat globules in solution.

Enough white stuff to paint
the telescope umpteen times over.

*

Grass builds an urgent layer of cells,
survives the night.

Cows bellow from another continent.
Cows are deeper than I care to think.

    *

We are thirsty creatures, snout round
the muddy edges of the waterhole,
compelled to do this, to approach
the narrow door in the spectrum,
our whole bodies quivering
at the possibility of water.

    *

Deaf and blind to most of what goes on
I point my white stick at the sources out there
and tingle as currents begin to travel.
If *only* I could see it, the white radio sky –
or some colour I can't describe, bright though –
with live connections I could turn up
the gain and make some sort of purchase on,
like double-fisted chords felt fortissimo in the ground

but it's hard work, always probing the world's outline
where nothing is given for sure
except that walking between traffic gets harder.

    *

Mine's the only car in the car park.
A film crew returns to their van
for the long drive south
but there are no crowds,
it is 4 o'clock, Friday.

Grass darkens. Lights are on
in the labs where last e-mails are sent

and a lost jumper tracked down
before its owner goes on holiday.

*

The telescope knows no sympathies,
must accept whatever labels I give it.
All it takes is twilight, shadows,
and I can fill the bowl with long dead pulsars,
globular clusters and star speed.
                    Or farther out,
flash and counter-flash, high energy civilisation,
annihilation, wellspring and sink,
creatures swimming past death and being born,
bat-flight plummet and brake
scribbling my name on the sky in invisible ink.

This poem does not fill a sky.

Beyond the control room,
the eyes of the cows are unfathomable,
squirrels nibble at the immensity
and grass spreads far
across the Cheshire Plain.